About the author

Graham Andrews is a professional writer living on the South Coast of New South Wales. He has worked as a scientific editor, technical writer, freelance writer and writing tutor. He is the author of ten books.

Easy Guide
to
Creative
Writing

Graham J Andrews

Flairnet

First published 2014

ISBN 978-0-9924642-1-9

Published by Flairnet
www.flairnet.com.au
Post Office Box 645
Narooma NSW 2546
Australia

National Library of Australia Cataloguing-in-Publication entry
Author: Andrews, Graham J., author.
Title: Easy guide to creative writing / Graham J Andrews.
ISBN: 9780992464219 (paperback)
Subjects: Creative writing--Handbooks, manuals, etc.
Dewey Number: 808.02

Contact the author:
Website: www.grahamandrews.com
Email: graham@grahamandrews.com

Contents

Introduction

Everyone has a story to tell. Creative writing is all about the human experience. But those stories should only be told if they are interesting, hold the reader's attention and perhaps imagination, and are truly worthy of telling. How do you develop the skill to write a story that is compelling reading?

Many writers of fiction find it very difficult to get their works published by magazines or publishers. I don't tell them it's easy, because it's not. But I encourage people to write if they have that passion to put words down and create a story—their story.

Develop those writing skills you probably thought were lying there, asleep. Now's the time to wake them up and put them to good use. This *Easy Guide To Creative Writing* will take you through the art of writing fiction—short stories or your novel. You will learn how to develop a plot that will take your characters wherever you want them to go. Develop your characters. Create real people. They will work, they will have relationships, sometimes broken relationships, sometimes happy ones. They will have hobbies, they will be big or small, tall or short. Readers will be able to say, 'That sounds like Uncle Don ... '

Make your characters do exactly as you tell them. They will live, and breathe, just like real people. They will speak like real people. Make your characters old fashioned. Make them sexy. Vibrant. Devious. Unscrupulous. Make them loveable. Make them bore people in their environment. Make them stimulate those around them. Make them ... well, it's your story.

Your characters must say something. Well, modern characters usually say lots. But it's how they speak that can convey so much information to the reader. Proper dialogue actually tells the reader something important, and moves the story along.

All stories take place within a setting. Where is your story set? Is it a historic country town? Or squashed into a tiny corner of some horrible, smoky, filthy city?

Develop a setting your readers will be able to relate to. Bring your characters into the setting. Make them do something—let them all fight amongst themselves. Let them set goals. Let them do whatever you want them to do. This is where the action begins. It's the plot, or the story. And it is here too that you can really let your mind run away with your story.

Your first draft will probably need a lot of work to make it tidy, the sentences crisp and short. You will want to improve the punctuation, remove those loose ends, and the weakness of the characters you created. Edit your story and turn it into a literary masterpiece.

This book, like the others in the series, does not depend on endless exercises. The author considers many such exercises a waste of time, as it is most unlikely that any book, no matter how massive, will contain just the right exercises that a writer will need in writing a particular piece of writing. Instead, it concentrated on the writer's story. This book also assumes a certain degree of understanding of the English language—the normal grammar rules and so on, without which you will have endless difficulties writing anything.

Chapter 1 *What's It All About?*

Creative writing is all about human experience. It is about cultural values. It is about how the writer sees something in his or her society, or imagines how it could be. Because all fiction—short story or novel—is the creation of an individual, it should be unique. Yes, there are many love stories, murders, tragedies, dramas in life portrayed through literature, but each story has a unique element. That element is the writer's input.

But before we even start, let's put writing—good writing—into perspective.

Most good writing is merely re-writing. You start with a draft, no matter how bad, and you make it good. Very few writers can write well on their first go. Their masterpiece is the result of frequent re-writes, edits, and further re-writes to get it to the high standard where the world reads their compositions and says, 'wow! That's truly wonderful. I wish I could write like that.' And how do they write so well? As I mentioned ... by re-writing. A good writer will make the end result of their effort look easy, but most likely, it was far from easy, full of frustration and disappointment.

Once you have written that first draft, there's often hours of work ahead of you—as there is for the world's very best writers. The writing—to produce the first draft, is one thing. The main thing is in the re-writing, because that is the effort that is going to pay you well, and result in that hidden genius that is just waiting to come into the real world.

Do you want to become a writer? Of course you do. So how good a writer do you want to become? Well, it depends on how often you are prepared to re-write your work, and edit it, and rewrite ...

Good writing comes from being prepared to throw out that early draft because it didn't lead you to where you hoped it would go. Good writing comes from patience, endless patience, and believing that you can turn that first draft into a masterpiece. Writing and re-writing are almost inseparable. One can't exist without the other.

If you think your first draft is not very good, feel better in knowing that nearly all the great writers in the world felt the same way about their first drafts. But with patience, with determination to reach their goal of becoming a good writer—

indeed the best writer—they re-wrote as often as their goals dictated.

And only then did they try to get their work into print!

Now, having got all misunderstanding out of the way, let's get on with looking at the writing process.

Literature can show you things you have never seen before and will never forget.

In writing fiction, like all other forms of writing, it is necessary to learn a few simple rules. If you know what you are doing, you can break these rules. Most writers do!

Creative writing is a portrait of life, or a portrait of a small portion of a life, a few minutes or perhaps a few days taken from a person's life, with all sorts of events and people woven around those moments, no matter how long a time they span. But such time excerpts should not be so trite or trivial that a reader could say that they were taken from some newspaper, the article conceived by a journalist who lacked imagination about the possibilities in the real world, where he could have described events that could have happened, or people who might have lived.

This doesn't mean that the creative writer can't make up the story, or the characters, or the scene. After all, that's what creative writing is about—creating events and characters and putting them together to make them do something interesting.

It is the originality of a story, and of the characters, that readers want, not a regurgitation of some worn-out story rehashed many times over by writers who don't, and can't, develop originality for themselves.

Nevertheless, that time excerpt should be believable, except perhaps in the case of science fiction or fantasy, where just about anything out of this world is allowed to happen, indeed, is encouraged to happen!

There is one thing all creative writers should believe, even if it is the only fact in writing fiction. When you sit down to write, as a writer you should do so not because you have to tell a story, but because you have a particular story to tell. And that story must really want to be told. It must be told. It has to be told. Then, and only then, is it a good time to start writing!

Virtually all fiction (science fiction, romance, suspense, fantasy, adventure, western or anything else you want to write about) follows a formula, but make sure you never tell an editor you are creating formula writing! That's definitely a no-no when it comes to getting your works published. But basically, that magic formula is simply writing about experiences editors want for their readers. Writers who give editors what their readers want will attain greater success than if they do not follow this simple formula.

Editors claim to know their readers well. So, in creating your story, you really write it for the editor. Please him or her, and you will please all your other readers. Sounds simple, doesn't it? Many readers do not want literary masterpieces that are going to win prizes for the obscure messages they contain. So write it for the editor, and for your intended readers! The average reader reads only to be entertained. What the reader wants has not varied much over time.

The best way to improve your own writing is to read lots of other stories. Don't read only stories you like. Read stories you think are terrible, and ask yourself why you thought they were terrible. It's like watching terrible television. It is much easier to find fault with something that is bad, rather than finding praise for something you like, unless that is obvious. And then apply your criticism to your own stories when you have finished them.

Having a thousand good ideas in your head is no good. You have to get them on paper. Just sit down and do it. Begin. Don't worry about what the first draft looks like. That can generally be fixed up in the heavy editing when you have finished the draft. The important thing, as a new writer, is to get those ideas of yours down on paper.

You will get your ideas down, develop those new ideas, and turn them into a plot that interests readers. And then, by improving your work, hopefully get it published.

Chapter 2 Getting Ideas

Ideas are the starting point for any writing—fiction, non-fiction, or whatever else you wish to write. Ideas are everywhere. Some of them come naturally but it's worth knowing where to look for that extra piece of inspiration. Life is full of ideas, useful characters, in fact everything you need to begin that short story or novel.

Try browsing through newspapers. Look for different stories, not just the politics and economic news that feature largely in the daily press.

Listen to other people's conversations. Listen in on conversations if you can get away with it. People are always telling each other their secrets. Perhaps their whisperings make the start of a really good story.

Look at other stories you have enjoyed. Consider the ideas for a plot. Remember, there's no copyright on an idea, just the finished product, so feel free to use someone else's ideas if you need to. But remember there is copyright on those other stories.

Look at everything that happens in your world. Even small incidents can have a story if you combine the incident with a vivid imagination.

Whatever your source of ideas, this is just the starting point for a story.

But remember, with many writers, life cannot provide them with plots. Personal events might have no significance to the stories they want to tell. Sometimes, real life lacks plots. Think of many people you know. Do their lives have real plots you could base your characters on? Possibly not.

Chapter 3 The Elements of the Story

Most short stories and novels have the following theme: a likeable character overcomes conflict in their life by their own efforts. In other words, they resolve a conflict.

In fiction, nothing should happen at random. Every element in a story should have significance. Don't add elements just because you like them! Names, places, actions and events should all be purposeful.

The story is really the collection of the plots of its individual characters.

Each character has a personal agenda, modified by conflict or concordance with the agendas of others.

The main ingredients of fiction are:

- Plot or conflict—this is the part of the story that gets characters involved with one another, and often against one another. It's the part of the story that makes it interesting!

- Character(s)—without them, you don't have a story to tell. Characters interact, and they provide the conflict, while others try to resolve the conflicts that other characters find themselves involved in.

- Dialogue—we all say something. Some people talk all the time in real life, others say very little. Dialogue has to be true to form, in others words, the style of dialogue has to be consistent with the character talking.

- Setting—this is where the story is set, the period in which the story is set, and the physical side of the story, whether it is in a big city, in an office, or in an aeroplane flying over the city somewhere.

- Theme—this is like the message you are conveying to your readers, and what you want to achieve by telling your story.

- Style—this is how you are going to tell your story. It is the actual language that makes the whole story work. Style exists in the writing itself, and is a combination of how you write, including the words, the sentences, the paragraphs. It is an extension of your own voice, but spoken through the story you are telling.

Chapter 4 The Plot

The plot, or the storyline, is where you can introduce conflict or whatever you want to make it.

Conflict is really the wrong person being in the wrong place at the wrong time.

Consider a boss who is given a promotion. No big deal, really.

But what would happen if, through some strange circumstances, a junior was promoted to the managerial position instead of the one who could rightfully claim the position? Now you have some conflict. This young person could wreak havoc with the place. He could feel so out of his depth that he can't cope, and neither can his staff, many of whom could be many years his senior. Now this is getting interesting.

And what if that person fabricated his résumé just to get the job? (oh, yes, it does happen!). And what if he is now about to be found out?

Do you see how easy it is to create conflict? Just put the person in the wrong place.

But conflict can arise from interactions with animals. If your character does not like dogs, and the woman's new friend is passionate about dogs, then there also is conflict. How do they resolve the issue? Who will win? And you can keep the tension going. If the woman simply says, 'I can't stand your dog. Goodbye.' Well, end of story. Your story must have more than such an abrupt ending. The issue must be resolved.

A short story will have only one plot, one that is well defined and clear to the reader. The plot is the reason for the story. Although a good plot is essential to the story, on its own it won't keep the story moving forward if the characters are weak, their dialogue boring.

A story with no plot is no story at all. A plot gives rise to scenes that bring out personalities. Indeed, the plot often makes the character. The plot also is the reason for revealing the character.

A plot is the story's skeleton around which the characters revolve. The plot provides a conflict or an obstacle that tests the main character. This conflict develops and the conflict should be resolved.

The Plot

Conflict can be relatively ordinary and recognisable, or dramatic. Whatever its nature depends on the genre of the story. Science fiction, for example, is likely to have a more bizarre conflict than a romantic story.

Although at first many writers think that conflict is just … well, conflict, there are three main types of conflict. We have the individual against himself or herself (very common); the individual against another individual (also very common), and the individual against forces of nature.

These forces may be virtually anything beyond the character's control, such as the weather, disasters natural or otherwise, war, large multinational corporations, the government, corruption ...

If you write, 'boy meets girl,' there is no plot for a story. But by writing, 'They despised each other from their first moment together. But it was going to get worse,' you have provided at least the start of a plot for a story.

The plot draws the reader into your characters' lives and helps the reader understand the choices that the characters make.

WHAT GOES INTO A PLOT?

Tradition requires writers to develop stories with particular plot elements in place. These include:

- Exposition: the information needed to understand a story. It is an expression of the mind of the writer, and is constructed logically according to how we think, and how we feel. It is cause and effect, positive and negative, the impact one point told has on the next. Exposition gives the reader the background to the characters, so the reader better appreciates why they may act the way they do, or speak the way they do.

- Complication: the catalyst that begins the major conflict. This either starts the conflict as a catalyst, or helps develop an existing conflict further.

- Climax: the turning point in the story that occurs when characters try to resolve the complication. This is the part of the story that resolves the conflict, putting everything right for the characters.

- Resolution: the set of events that bring the story to a close. This is the part that gives many stories their happy ending.

The Plot

Fiction must never be predictable. If it is, it's boring. *Zzzzzzzz!* Remember that fiction is very much like real life—it's seldom a straight line from the beginning to the end.

Foreshadow all-important elements. An important character, location, or object should be foreshadowed early in the story. You can't pull a rabbit out of your hat to rescue your hero, so always plan well ahead and put in place (or at least mention the existence of) those mysterious forces that are going to save the world, or at least your heroine, from certain death.

A short story is a self-contained work of fiction. Nothing should go before it. Nothing else should be intermixed with it. Nothing should follow after it, if it is not related to the story that is being told.

Chapter 5 Point of View

Ask witnesses at the scene of a fire exactly what happened before you arrived at the scene. You will get a different point of view from each one, even though each saw the same thing. Each witness will place more emphasis on one aspect rather than another, depending on his or her values, depending on what's really important in that person's mind. So with a dozen witnesses to the event, you can have a dozen stories to tell, each from a different point of view. In telling a story, you, the writer, must pick the point of view that works best for the idea you are creating. Later on, you will find that if you change your point of view (that is, the person telling the story, or moving it along), you can change the whole story beyond imagination.

In fiction, who tells the story (point of view) and how that person tells it are important issues for a writer to decide. Someone is always there between the reader and what is happening in the story. The tone, the feel of the story, and even its meaning, can change, depending on who is telling the story. That person is telling the story from his or her own point of view. This angle from which the people, events and details of a story are viewed, is important to consider when reading—and telling—a story.

The viewpoint character must be present at main events. He or she must be actively involved in the story and not just a chance observer. He or she should have a personal stake in the outcome of the story even if the outcome depends on the main character's actions.

Ask yourself: have you chosen the best person to tell the story? Is this character in a position to see the main events of the story? Will the character be affected by them?

There is always more than one side to any tale. Take the time to develop your characters, then determine who can best tell the story you want to write.

Let's look now at the main types of point of view.

OBJECTIVE POINT OF VIEW

With the objective point of view, the writer tells what happens without stating more than can be inferred from the story's action and dialogue. The narrator never discloses anything about what the characters think or feel, instead always remaining a detached observer.

THIRD PERSON POINT OF VIEW

This is the most common point of view used by writers. A story using this point of view is usually told in the past tense. The author tells the story solely through the eyes of one, or sometimes two, main characters and the focus should not shift from character to character within any given scene.

The narrator is not one of the characters, but lets us know exactly how the characters feel. We learn about the characters through this outside voice.

The person telling the story from a point of view must seem to be present, watching the action, almost as if unobserved by the characters. We can't have the characters becoming self-conscious because they know every movement, every word they say is being reported, can we?

One of the problems is the person can only report what is happening, as if they are present. But there are ways we can get around that.

Let's consider an argument taking place in a room. The person narrating the story gets up, says 'I am going to buy some cigarettes. I've had enough of this pettiness.' How do we know what has happened in that room during his absence? We simply get one of the other characters who was present in the room to tell him what took place. 'There was a serious accident near the shops,' he told them on his return. 'Well, we had our own dramas here,' replied Monica. 'While you were away, we were fighting fires because the photocopier caught fire and the flames extended to the paper storeroom next door. You can probably smell the smoke.'

By using tactics such as this, we have continuity of story, even in the absence of the character telling the story.

FIRST PERSON POINT OF VIEW

In the first person point of view, the narrator does participate in the action of the story. When reading stories in the first person, we need to realize that what the narrator is recounting might not be the objective truth. We should question the trustworthiness of the accounting.

One of the characters tells the story in the 'I' voice. This viewpoint can provide powerful emotional insight and connection.

There are drawbacks to writing in the first person, though. When writing about the 'I' character, you are limited to only what that person sees, thinks or learns. Nevertheless, a good writer can make it work very effectively.

Another drawback with first-person narrators is that they are not always trustworthy. It's very much like reading an autobiography. Sometimes (often, perhaps?) the narrator only reveals what he or she wants the readers to know; they will cover up all the saucy bits, and embellish the heroic stuff in their lives.

LIMITED OMNISCIENT POINT OF VIEW

In this type of point of view, a narrator who knows everything about all the characters is all knowing, or omniscient. A narrator whose knowledge is limited to one character, either major or minor, has a limited omniscient point of view.

THIRD PERSON MULTIPLE (OR AUTHOR OMNISCIENT)

This point of view is popular with fantasy writers, where a large cast of characters is used, or in works where a narrator relates parts of the story, but the story as a whole is told through the eyes of several major characters, often shifting points of view at each chapter or scene change. This type of point of view has the benefit of showing the reader what is happening with other sub-plots and lesser characters before the hero knows about it.

Chapter 6 Setting for Your Story

Where's the story taking place? In an office? A city, perhaps?

With creative writing, you, as writer, are not compelled to stick with the known, like home, town, office.

Try something different, perhaps even out of this world. There are hundreds of millions of stars in hundreds of billions of galaxies for you to choose from. There's the ocean, or boats bobbing up and down on the waves.

There's also just the two seats of the car. A family going somewhere. Where, and what, could be the plot of the story, where you can introduce lots of conflict and tension. And with whom?

So for your story, you will create the setting. But you will describe it in the smallest detail, because if you don't know your setting that closely, you will find it difficult to make the characters behave as you want them to.

So in your description of setting, don't leave anything out.

If you need to ask yourself even one question '… I wonder if the car is blue or black, a recent model, or an old bomb …'

then you will not have included enough information for yourself. If you need to ask yourself even one question, you can be sure your readers will ask ten questions.

But it's only by knowing where your story takes place, that you can make the story really work.

Every story would be different if its characters were elsewhere and plot happened somewhere else. Fiction depends on where it is set—its locality. Writers write about what they know, with sights, sounds, colours, and feelings all described vividly. The location of a story's actions, and the time in which the action occurs, is the setting.

Setting is created by words and descriptions. Readers know about the setting, where all the actions are taking place, and where the characters are at any particular time, through the words of the writer. How much the reader learns is up to the writer. Many authors leave such details for their readers to picture.

You can organise the setting progressively. For example, your story is set on the coast. Describe the general coastline, then you can home in on the details:

'The several headlands stretched in never-ending curves towards the northern horizon. Closer to where Baz was standing, the rocks were particularly jagged, dwarfing those washed smooth by the pounding waves on the next headland. Hilda's home was that small hazy dot on the last prominent headland. Her home was even more distant than the lighthouse on the distant island he could just make out through the sea mist. So far from her, he must have realised. So many hours on horseback to reach her home. Just below where he was standing were a series of small rock pools, filled from time to time by the wash of the waves. These did not experience the roaring power of the erosive breakers further along the exposed beaches and headlands. And between those pools, small sand drifts broke up an otherwise continuous line of ruggedness.'

From this, you are giving your readers an overall picture of the coastline, with at least some perspective of scale, and then you are homing in on smaller and smaller sections of it, to those small parts of the whole that the character could see. Stand back from the general scene as you describe it, unless you are a character in the story and you need to describe it from a personal point of view. And in describing a landscape, don't become a tour guide! Most readers would be familiar with boring descriptions written by writers lacking imagination. If you can include further details, such as 'the limestone cliffs ...', the reader knows the cliffs are white, and might be steep due to the erosion they would have suffered from the ocean.

Sometimes characters react to what they see. The scene evokes emotion. No matter how much reaction from the character, the reader must be able to picture the scene, right down to its last little detail. The reader must also be there, looking, taking in each of those headlands, rock pools or sand drifts.

And if the description of the scene is as Baz would see it, then his mood can be conveyed through the prose. If he were frightened, then the scene would be frightening; if he is intimidated by the enormity of the landscape, then he might feel insignificant out there. The description of the landscape is coloured by how Baz sees it, or how he reacts to it. The description can really be an impression of what the person sees, how he sees it.

If you, as a writer, are creating an impression, you must appeal to the readers' senses. Charge the descriptions, and thus the impressions, with emotion. Try to arouse in your reader feelings like your own.

WHAT SETTING TELLS US

A description of a setting can add value to the setting as a whole. A description of a run-down farmhouse could tell us that the whole area is poor, and its inhabitants have little future.

Setting can add meaning, reflecting the characters' behaviour and thus developing the theme of the story.

Whether your story takes place on an imaginary world or right here on present-day earth, setting is a crucial part of any story. How you build the world around your characters will play a vital role in the overall believability of your story. The type of world you create will determine the reactions and behaviours of your characters.

Chapter 7 Characters

Develop the characters you might include in your short story.

You will have to make these people special. You will have them obey every command you give them. If they don't, you will want to know why they go their own way. Perhaps it's because they have very strong personalities, and won't be told anything.

Make them up. This is creative writing, so here's your chance to create the real people you want. They can be horrible, nasty, greedy, brutal … whatever you want to make them.

But before they will do what you want them to do in your story, you must know them perhaps better than you know your own family members.

You will want to know what they look like. Are they tall? Short? Thin? Do they walk with a stoop?

What is their appearance? That is, how do they dress? What will they be wearing during your story?

How do they talk? Is their speech fast or slow? Do they talk in groups of only a few words, instead of speaking in a fluent manner?

Are they intelligent? Are they boring? Are they real leaders or followers?

What sort of work do they do? Do they like doing that type of work? What would they prefer to be doing?

Are they busy people, always on the move? Or are they lazy?

You might think this is too much to write into your characters, but knowing all there is to know about them is important if you want them to take the part that you intended for them in your story. Without knowing your characters intimately, you won't be able to work with them very easily, and they will not show themselves up as true to type.

You must know the people you are working with.

The characters you create don't have to be real people. But they could be. They might even be your work colleagues that you would like to carve up and mutilate for the way they have treated you at work. This is your way of perhaps changing your perception of those people, or ... perhaps doing what you want to with them, but in a socially acceptable way.

Characters

We all know people. We work with them. We mix with them after work. We catch the bus with them. We see other people during our lunch breaks. Many such people are just ordinary people with ordinary lives. But each one could be a potential character. Put a story around each person you meet. You sit next to someone on the bus. Weave a story around that person while they sit next to you. Let your mind run wild.

Try thinking of the shoppers you meet at the supermarket in a different way. What could they be like? Are they what they seem to be to you? With your mind running wild, they could be anything. They could be fantastic lovers. They could be criminals pretending to be 'normal' people. They could be dull workmates. Your characters in fiction could, really, be anything you want them to be.

Get to know everything you can about your characters. Think of their pasts, their family, their occupations, hobbies. Consider their upbringing, for upbringing will influence how a person turns out in later life. What is their physical appearance? You may never use all the information you have created about them but your characters will be more real, the more vivid you make them.

Look out for characters when you meet someone. Watch their actions. Listen to what they say and how they say it. How do they relate to others? How do other people relate to them? Look for ideas you might be able to include in your story.

LEARNING ABOUT YOUR CHARACTERS

Characters are usually people, but not always. The story could be about a dog, a cougar, or even elves. Does a character have to be a person? Can it be a lion stalking its next victim, or can it be a cyclone? The story could even be about a machine. A computer perhaps, that seems to have a mind of its own. Not very original, I know, but you get the message, I am sure!

Most stories have one main character, perhaps more in a longer work of fiction. Other characters are always minor characters.

Readers learn about the characters you create in many ways. These are descriptions of their physical traits, and by their dialogue, and actions.

Characters can be made individual by the clothes you put on them, and by the opinions you give them. Listen to individuals speak. Listen to them at work, or in a shopping centre or mall. What they say, how they say it, will tell you more about them than if they were to describe themselves to you.

You too can tell your readers so much more about your characters by making them say things, than you can by making them do things. Their conversation is really a reflection of their inner feelings and inner thoughts. It is this, the inner workings of your characters, that you want to develop for your readers. This is what the characters are all about, how they feel inside, what they are made of, and what they think, believe.

Are there any limits to who can be a character in your story? Definitely not. Think of a real life situation, perhaps a scene in your office, or in a restaurant. There are males and females, some are rich, others poor, some are young, others old. Their backgrounds are as varied as those people in your office or in the restaurant. But what is important is that the characters all have real emotions, just as your reader does. They are happy or sad, they could be down in the dumps, they can express disappointment, pain, joy, and love, just like you can. In others words, your characters must seem real.

Plausible, complex characters are crucial to successful storytelling. You can develop them in several ways. Creating a believable character requires that you know them inside and out. If you don't know your characters then how can you convey who they are to your readers?

Make your characters insecure! Give your characters some conflict. And how do you develop conflict? By putting a person in the wrong environment! The story develops by the character(s) reacting to their environment.

When developing a story idea, the first step is to decide what type of character you need to make the plot work. Once you have your story idea in mind, it's time to flesh out those characters. What does your character look like? Her taste in clothes, physical flaws, birthmarks, tattoos. How does she behave? Does she have pet expressions, gestures, mannerisms? Is she quick to anger or does she withdraw from conflict? How does your character speak?

Dialogue can kill a good novel if it's too hard to follow, but this is more than just accent. Does your character use flowery prose to describe the simplest of things? Does he use a minimum of words? How does your character interact with other characters? Is he kind and giving? Does he allow himself to be walked on or is he prickly and standoffish?

Characters

All characters have specific homes, possessions, medical histories, tastes in furniture, political opinions. You can express a character's nature metaphorically through objects or settings (a rusty sword, an apple orchard in bloom, a violent thunderstorm). The character's speech (both content and manner) helps to evoke personality: shy and reticent, aggressive and frank, coy, humorous. Both content and manner of speech should accurately reflect the character's social and ethnic background without stereotyping.

From table manners to performance in hand-to-hand combat, each new example of behaviour should be consistent with what we already know of the character, yet it should reveal some new aspect of personality. Behaviour under different forms of stress should be especially revealing.

The characters should have good and sufficient reasons for their actions, and should carry those actions out with plausible skills. If we don't believe characters would do what the writer tells us they do, the story fails.

One useful way to learn more about your characters is to fill out a detailed profile for them, at least for the more important ones. You may not use all this information, but nevertheless the information will help you.

Chapter 8 Dialogue in Fiction

You have developed your characters. Now make them say a few things. Anything, just to see how they talk.

It's not easy. But what sometimes helps is if you imagine your character in front of another person, just the two of them talking together. Picture yourself creeping up to them and listening in on their conversation as if they don't even know you are present. Now that's the way you should make your characters talk. Nothing forced. Nothing contrived. Just … natural conversation.

For now, forget about the setting or the plot. Just put each of your characters in front of another person and let them talk. And listen to them.

This should be the easiest part of writing, and the most interesting part too, because it is in the dialogue that you give your characters their personalities, that is further brought out by the setting, or situation in which they find themselves. Unfortunately speech looks different when it is written down.

Dialogue in Fiction

Dialogue has to sound like speech. Speak your dialogue out aloud; if it doesn't sound natural, revise it.

Good dialogue has several functions:

- To tell us, through the conversations of the characters, what we need to know to make sense of the story;

- Convey character: to show us what kinds of people we're dealing with;

- Convey a sense of place and time: to evoke the speech patterns, vocabulary and rhythms of specific kinds of people;

- Develop conflict: to show how some people use language to dominate others, or fail to do so.

- Dialogue is more that just talking. It is reacting to what another has said.

Good dialogue depends on making it as natural as possible. Normal conversation is not generally grammatically perfect. It is full of ums and ers and other irritations the listeners become used to. Sentences are often left incomplete. However, if you 'write as it is spoke', you won't have many readers finishing your stories. They will lose interest after the fourth um and second er and the fifth pause. Find the balance between written English and conversational English. Know your characters. Know what they would say and how they would say it. Listen to people around you speaking. I mean really listen to them.

THE PURPOSE OF DIALOGUE

Dialogue communicates something, either to the reader or to another character within the story. But whatever is said, dialogue must drive the story forward. Don't let your characters say something just to fill in space on a white page.

We all know how boring people can be if they just say something to fill the vacuum of silence.

It doesn't work like that in fiction. There is no room in any form of writing, especially fiction, for unnecessary words. If you don't have a genuine reason to include them, take them out. If the words don't move the story forward, don't include those words!

Dialogue is a crucial part of every character. The way they speak and what they say can be as revealing as a physical description. But make sure it is your character speaking, not yourself, with your tone, your voice coming across to the readers. If you have something important to say to the reader, by all means say it through your characters but let it be in their voice. Readers do not like being lectured.

Dialogue alters the pace of a story. Short sentences without narrative increase the pace, long speeches slow it down. Use dialogue to increase the tension, action or suspense in your story.

WRITING DIALOGUE

Make it natural. Well, natural for each character. Avoid writing phonetically ('wrote as it is spoke'). It is distracting to the reader and quite unintelligible. If you wish a character to have an accent, simply tell the readers they have one. The rhythm of their speech will convey this much better than a lot of unintelligible words you have invented for the occasion.

WHO SAID WHAT AND HOW

Use 'he said' or 'she said' to attribute speech to a particular character, but don't overdo it. If you tell the readers who starts off the conversation, and with whom, you don't need to repeat he said, she said, he said. You can improve the method of attributing speech to particular characters by using phrases such as 'she snapped', 'he whispered', 'he murmured'. Use such phrases sparingly. Well-written dialogue should convey how the words were said without the need for any of the above.

Avoid long blocks of dialogue, and include the occasional indicator of who is speaking so the reader does not lose track of where the dialogue is up to. Include someone's name into the dialogue. This is the simplest way of telling readers which character's turn it is to speak. 'Do you agree with me now, Sue?'

SHOW OR TELL?

This can be brought out in dialogue, such as waiting for the 8.00 train that is late! Make dialogue like radio dialogue— every word must tell the listener (reader) something.

Have your character say, 'Damn. This train should have been here thirty minutes ago. It's always late.' This is better than saying 'He looked at his watch. It was 8.30 a.m. He paced up and down the platform, sneaking a look at his watch as he did so. He was angry.

Action as well as speech is a part of dialogue. We expect to know when the speakers pause, where they're looking, what they're doing with their hands, how they respond to one another. The characters' speech becomes just one aspect of their interactions; sometimes their words are all we need, but sometimes we definitely need more.

Chapter 9 Themes in Fiction

The theme of a piece of fiction is its view about life and how people behave. Yet it is a very subtle element of all fiction, an underlying element running right through the story. It is one of those magical properties of fiction that is not really described, but is present. Its readers are aware of it. It is something that is relayed to the readers through the characters, the action and setting that make up the story. The theme of a story is that ingredient that the readers perceive for themselves.

FINDING THE THEME

Sometimes the title tells readers a lot about the theme. Patterns described in the fiction may indicate a theme, meanings—hidden and obvious—are indicators of theme.

Remember that theme, characters, plot and structure are inseparable. Together they help to inform the reader, and they reflect back on each other. On its own, a theme never completely explains the story. It is simply one of the elements that make up the whole, just like the characters, the plot and the dialogue do in their own ways.

Chapter 10 Style

The secret of style is not in having everything so perfect that you would score full marks in an examination for your grammar. This would result in writing that is so dead it should be immediately buried. It's the little imperfections in how actions are carried out ... how things are said ... Otherwise your style would be like a worn-out coin, with all the images rubbed away with correctness, with no crispness left to make the story interesting. Aim for perfection with your writing; don't always aim for perfection of the rules in the way you tell your story.

Avoid using foreign phrases. Not everyone understands Italian. Or Greek. So don't use words your readers won't understand.

Try varying your sentence length. Use short sentences. Two words might do. Perhaps three. Use long sentences to vary the pace of the story, especially if the particular scene is moving slowly. Aim for crispness. Aim for originality. And for freshness. Start some sentences with 'and'. Or 'but'. But don't of course overdo this style. Overuse leads to a boring style, exactly what you are trying to avoid by varying the narrative. Aim for something more original and inspiring than boring public-service style narrative. While that might be 'well-written' and correct in a grammatical sense, it might not keep the reader awake late into the night.

Introduce uncommon words, but not too many of them. If your reader doesn't understand a lot of unusual words or phrases, he won't enjoy the story you are trying to tell. But on the other hand, aim for something that is more than just a string of the commonly used words and phrases. Remember, we have heard them all before, probably many times over. Pick something in between these extremes for an interesting style.

I sometimes run the 'find' function of my computer over my writing. Pick some words that you have used a few times, and see just how often those words are repeated. And then go and change most of them if the count is quite high. See how many sentences start with '. And ' and change some if the total is high. By asking your computer to find the full stop, space and the And, you will be asking it to find all sentences beginning with that word. Then repeat the procedure for But, and so on if you have doubts about other frequently used words.

Chapter 11 Writing Your Story

Let's begin by looking at your short story.

In the first couple of paragraphs—no more—the reader will want to know the following things.

Who is your main character? What is this person like? Can the reader identify with this character? He doesn't have to be present. The other characters could be expecting him shortly. They could be talking about him, or his arrival, so readers will know of his existence.

Where is the story set? At least give readers a clue about setting. Details can be filled in as the story progresses, perhaps through actions of the characters, plot and so on.

When is all the action happening? As readers have a right to know so they can picture appropriate action in their minds as they read, the time of the setting is critical to the readers' appreciation of what you have written.

What kind of story are you telling? You should establish the mood of your story early in the writing, so the reader knows whether this is a funny, serious, romance, thriller or whatever story you have created.

Most readers know what they want to read, and they expect a particular type of story. So make sure you don't create a half-and-half story, that is one that begins by being serious and turns into humour. Humour does have its place, but only if appropriate to a particular character.

When you begin, you must capture the reader's attention in the first paragraph. If your reader is bored or disappointed with your first paragraph, you have lost that person and won't get him or her back to read the rest, unless they are desperate and bored and they will read anything just to fill in a few minutes. And if the editor is disappointed with your first paragraph, your story will not be published. Either don't waste your time writing at all, or better still, make sure paragraph one stands out. It's simple advice, isn't it?

Show one or more characters under some kind of appropriate stress. For example, if the hero must perform well under enemy fire in the climax, show him being shot at in Chapter One, and performing badly. If the heroine must resist temptation at the end, show her (or someone else) succumbing to temptation in the beginning.

Show us who's the 'good guy,' who's the 'bad guy'. That is, in whom should we make an emotional investment? Whose side are we on? Even if the hero is morally repugnant (a hired killer, for example), he could nevertheless display some trait or attitude we can admire and identify with. The villain can be likeable but set on a course we must disapprove of.

Establish the setting—where and when the story takes place.

Establish the area of conflict. This can be reinforced in the setting.

Foreshadow the ending. The final gasp of the hero should be hinted at early in the story.

In the body of the story, tell your story in scenes, not in exposition. A scene contains a purpose, an obstacle or conflict, and a resolution tells us something new about the characters and their circumstances.

Develop your characters through action and dialogue. Show us, don't tell us, what's going on and why (not 'He was loud and rude', but 'Get outa my way, you jerk!' he bellowed'). The reader's imagination should be free to arouse feelings.

Include in the early stages of your story all the elements you need for your conclusion. The conclusion, or closing scenes, or resolution, should at least be present in a hidden way, near the beginning of your story.

Your characters need motivation for their actions and words. They need to be doing things for good reasons.

Develop the plot as a series of increasingly serious problems, where each stage in the plot develops and leads comfortably into the next scene, or stage of the story.

Keep your readers in suspense by making the options available to the main character uncertain.

And finally, make the solutions to the problems appropriate to the characters and in keeping with the personality and behaviour of your characters.

In the conclusion, present a climax, a final conflict when everything gained so far is in danger and could be lost by a single deed. This should reveal something to your readers which has been present from the outset but which did not stand out.

Throughout the story, remember that nothing in a story happens at random. Everything, every word, every action, every character, must have a purpose in your story.

THE CONCLUSION

Most stories are decided on the first page, and often in the first one or two paragraphs. Imagine the poor editor reading something that does not interest him. If the editor simply cannot get interested in your story to continue reading, or is not satisfied with the outcome, or the resolution is not right, believable or interesting enough, he or she simply won't read any further. Always remember that yours is not the only story the editor has to contend with on that day yours arrives on his desk.

Create a good story the editor enjoys, and you can be pretty sure your other readers will enjoy your creation too. Who knows where your writing will take you?

BE CRITICAL OF YOUR STORY

Most elements of a good story are very obvious. Too obvious, perhaps, that's why many writers ignore them!

Your main character has to be doing something worthwhile—saving the world, saving himself from himself, or whatever you gave him life in your story to do. So make sure he does it, does it well, and relates well (or appropriately) to those around him.

Ask yourself what kind of person is your main character. Can your reader identify with that person, or even want to bother with such a person?

Consider the point of view. Who is going to tell the story for you, whose eyes is the action seen through? Consider first person, third person, or any other point of view that you think is best for your particular story.

Decide on the tone. Is it going to be a funny story, serious, thriller, romance, or some other style?

Where are you going to start your story? Unless you are writing an epic novel, don't start when the main character is born. Don't start by telling the readers about the weather. They're not interested in that unless there is a storm raging and the main character is fighting huge seas in a tiny boat. Make it more interesting that that. In reality, the plot begins long before the story begins. The short story itself should begin at the latest possible moment before the climax. In any situation or conflict, there is always a beginning before the major showdown. We may learn later, through flashbacks, exposition, or inference, about events occurring before the beginning of the story, if these are even necessary.

What are you trying to tell your readers? Don't moralise, don't pass judgement, don't criticise. Leave your readers to form an opinion about why they didn't like your character, be it he was a nasty person, got his justice in the end, met the right fate for such an undesirable character.

Chapter 12 Points to Ponder

Editors and publishers will buy a story or manuscript for these reasons:

- The story will give the readers what they expect.

- The story has a character (usually a likeable person) with whom the reader can identify.

- The main character solves their problems by their own efforts.

- The story makes the readers glad they read it, therefore giving the reader what they wanted from that magazine.

Your story or novel could be rejected for one of many reasons. Consider these reasons. They are all used at some time or other in the story-buying process magazines go through. The same reasons are given by book publishers.

- You probably sent the editor an unsolicited story. It is always advisable to send a query letter to the editor of a magazine first, to see if he or she really wants yet another story. Often magazine editors are swamped with stories from all over the country, and sometimes from all over world. They already have plenty to chose from. So ask if they want another one to consider. Tell them briefly about your story in no more than one page, but tell them why yours is going to be so much better that any they have already received so far. Here, concentrate more on the story, not about yourself generally, unless you are an up and coming story teller that most editors have already heard about. In that case, you could get away with concentrating on yourself more than on the story you are offering.

- You probably didn't send the story through a literary agent. Unfortunately, these days editors and publishers save time, and cut costs, by getting others do the work they used to do as part of their job. Now, they see the role of literary agent as the story sifter for them, sending them only those that are really great and that don't need much work. They receive only very few, compared with hundreds or perhaps thousands of stories over a year. I am sure you can see their point, but as a new writer, that's just one more obstacle in your path to success. And because you might not be well known in the publishing world, many literary agents do not take on previously unpublished writers, no matter how good they might be. After all ... no one has ever heard of them, so the editors, and publishers, and the readers of magazines and books haven't either. So how do you get your story accepted?

- It's not well written. Fair enough, you couldn't expect an editor to buy something that was sloppily put together, could you? The story you write must be the very best that anyone could possibly write. It must be free of all mistakes, free of ambiguities, and all those blemishes I have pointed out.

- The story does not meet her requirements. It is essential to look at the magazine's requirements to see just what they are publishing before wasting postage sending off your story to the wrong publication. Good writing does not compensate for bad choice of magazine. Don't send a romance story to an editor who wants Western stories, unless it has a romantic Western theme.

- Editors reject stories, no matter how well written they might be, because they feel that the particular story will not give their readers what they want or expect from that particular magazine. Editors know their magazines, and they know their readers. Many readers give them feedback, so over only a few issues, editors get a feel for what their readers want, and are looking for. How dare they give their readers anything else instead?

- The editor is merely the go-between the writer and the reader. He or she might act as a referee on the readers' behalf, and select stories they believe their readers will want to read. This is similar to the point above.

- The pace of the story was wrong. You might have tried to cram too much into the few pages available for a short story, or you really tried to write a condensed novel in six pages. Or it was too long for what you actually said. You must always check the pace and keep it consistent. It should be consistent with the theme, and the type of story, and the setting. Don't have a racy story set in a boring office, or a fast pace set at a yoga class. And don't have a story with a slow pace where the main character is fighting for his or her life. Your own feel for the story will help dictate the true pace you should aim for when telling your story.

- The story was not complete in itself. You left your readers up in the air as to what happened. Readers want to know if your main character was saved, lived to tell another story, or did something that was in keeping with his or her personality. Always make sure your conclusion is valid, and clear. But occasionally, you might write a story where the whole mystery of what happens is left up in the air for the reader to speculate. Sometimes, if this ending is justified, it can be effective. But make sure that it really is the ending you were hoping to achieve.

- You may have had character problems. This comes down to not really knowing all your characters. It might be that you don't know how they will act in the circumstances you put them into, or how they would react when confronted with one of the other characters, or with the weather. In real life, we all adapt, but some better than others. If we don't adapt to our situation, then that might be a reason for a problem with a character.

- Your main character might not have been real enough, or identifiable. Even if you create your characters, and with creative writing, there is much scope to do so, but to the reader, he or she has to consider them to be real, even with a bit of their imagination. If you are creating exceptional characters, then you have to work even harder for your reader to think of them in the same way that you did when you created them.

• Perhaps you had too many characters for a short story. Remember that if you have too many characters doing too much, readers soon lose track of who is doing what to whom. There is no real formula to say how many characters you should have for a certain number of pages. Use your discretion here, or your general feeling about how many people are just right. You can, of course, 'pool' a lot of characters, such as those in an office could speak with one voice, that voice telling the reader the thought, or thoughts, of the whole pool of characters. A school class, too, could act as 'the class', as a single character, rather than thirty or so children.

• The number of characters should be proportional to the length of the story. The longer the story, the more characters you are able to introduce safely. But please don't overdo the number of characters just because you like them. Put some of them into your next story! If your characters are really great, especially those you created for the occasion, but they don't really fit into a particular piece of writing, don't despair and think you have wasted your time. You probably haven't. A good writer can take any character, adapt them to another situation, and there they are in a new life. You might find that if your characters don't fit one story, you can create another story around those characters.

- The editor could not get interested enough in the characters to care what happened to them. Yes, there are stories like that, and television programs like that. They seem to be very ordinary people, leading very ordinary lives, in a very ordinary setting, doing very little. Write the story again with vigour next time!

- Nothing much happened in the story. You simply wrote a narrative about … well, nothing in particular, really. Unfortunately, even a well-written piece of fiction does not stand on its own. It has to convey something to the reader, something that makes the reader say, 'wow! I am glad I took the time to read that.'

- The characters did not have anything much to resolve, or did not resolve it by their own means. But a story about a person who has everything resolved for him could show him to be a rather weak, useless type, or one who has so much power in his circle that he commands such respect that all these things are done for him. Both these characters are viable in a well-written story that is set around them. The conflict comes about from their attitude, or their lack of attitude about anything, their lack of emotion. This, of course, comes down to how well you have developed your character, and your story. Both must be consistent with one another. They both must enhance one another, with plot and character working well together and enhancing what one offers to the other, whether the character enhances the plot, or vice versa.

- The story was just too depressing, too gruesome, littered with tragedy, blood and gore and corpses. Sometimes such stories do find a market, but check your market for such a story before you begin to write one with this type of theme. However, with changing social attitudes, and different generations of readers demanding differing things from their entertainment, this type of story could find a ready market in the very near future.

- The story was offensive. In other words, it was in very poor taste. You obviously haven't taken any notice of the style that a particular magazine wanted. Nor have you considered your potential readers. Give the readers, and the editor, or publisher, exactly what they want.

- The plot of your story is weak. This is a very common mistake, especially with writers early in their careers. The story might seem fine to the writer, but it is often wise to ask someone else who is completely honest with you, just what they think. But make sure you ask the right person to assess it. There are many, many people out there who would like to put someone else down because they are doing something they themselves would like to do, but can't. So make sure your assessor is well suited and honest.

- You have told it in a way that is unclear, confusing or offensive. Although you know what you are trying to say, doesn't mean that anyone else will get the same meaning, and make sense of what you are writing. Remember that you are only one person in the long chain of things that will lead to potential publication. Although the story might work for you, this is no guarantee that it will be received with the same enthusiasm by anyone else, least of all the editor or publisher. But then again, we all have different standards. And just because one person says it is terrible, this does not always mean that it really is all that bad. But it could be! It could be worse than the editor has told you, and he or she is merely being polite. So please assess the comments critically, and get someone else to criticise your writing also, to see if they too agree with the editor. Remember that editors are human, and suffer from the same faults and shortcomings as we all do.

- The editor couldn't read your story because it was typed with … and you forgot to put your name on it and … and … and … Please look at the check list included in this book! See if anything on that list is missing in your story.

- Your opening paragraph was too slow and the editor fell asleep before turning the page. This is a common fault. Fiction does not enjoy the luxury of slow starts. If it does, then it will have to be a very desperate editor who will publish a story that is so slow and painful in the beginning. After all, he will ask, when does the real story start? Perhaps it doesn't.

- The story simply grated on the editor's nerves and she hated it! Ask yourself why you sometimes turn off a movie that has been praised to the heavens, or throw down a short story or a book that has come from the pen (or more correctly these days, from the computer) of a famous story-teller. It's the same thing. A story that appeals to one person might have the opposite effect on the editor. Consider the editor's comments carefully before taking them to heart and brooding over the fact that the editor has told you, in effect, that you can't write. We all have bad days, and will be in a bad mood for any number of reasons. Perhaps this was the editor's off day. You can never tell what the other person was thinking, and you might, after all, having written something really great.

• Or simply, there just wasn't really a good reason why it was rejected. Sorry about that. We really are! Yes, I know, no reason might be a valid reason. We can't think of why we don't like it, but believe me, we don't like it. The reason could be hard to define. If this is the reaction from an editor, try revising the manuscript, or, better still, rewriting it from the very first word and see if the next draft is better. You could be surprised.

• The main character is not likeable enough. Your reader wants to be able to identity with the way in which your main character solves his or her problem. A nasty type will get his just treatment in the end, but it doesn't always happen in real life. But it could. If your readers could see that justice is done to your villain, the reader might begin to like him or her. A really nice person can go through hell and back again, but as long as all goes well for that character in the end, the reader will be happy, because the resolution was what they wanted. A final twist, a new direction for the character might be all that's needed to save the story. And the heroine.

- The odds are not insurmountable enough, or the editor does not believe they are sufficiently insurmountable. Don't fake the problem! Make it believable, make it real, even though the story is fiction. Yes, I realise that sounds like a bit of contradiction, but the character has to seem real, and the trials of life for him or her must seem real.

- The main character does not solve her problems by her own efforts. They are solved for her by one of the minor characters. Weak! This deprives the reader of the pleasure of feeling for the main character, admiring her after all she has gone through, just to find someone beat her to the resolution. We all look up to someone who can solve their own problems in life and come through a different, and stronger, person. In fiction, this applies equally well. So take out the character, or characters, who are always doing things for others, and make the person stand on their own two feet. But of course you could have a story about someone who is kind to others, and their friends like to pamper them, but you have to decide in your own story how far you can take this kindness. Take it too far, and the story disappears. Funny, that!

- The resolution is predictable, leaving nothing for the reader to get excited about. If the story is that predictable, why did you bother to write it? This is fiction, so the fiction can make you stretch the truth, and make you create a real story. So go ahead, and create that story.

- The goal is weak—there has to be real conflict that needs to be resolved. If it is too weak, the story just won't work. In fact, you probably won't even have a story! Again, you should ask yourself why you even bothered to write the story. Write it with a real story in mind. Make it exciting. Make it anything other than a boring, real-life soapy standard. Make it a really good story to tell.

And as a checklist for your own guidance, consider this list. For all the stories you write, ask yourself these questions:

Points to Ponder

- Is the title effective, appropriate and catchy?

- Does the short story or the novel work?

- Is it long enough to handle all the action and conflicts?

- Is it too long?

- Are there any unnecessary words?

- Are there any clichés?

- Would it appeal to the intended reader?

- Would the story hold their attention until the end?

- Would they think about the story after they have read it?

- Would they be able to relate to the story? Would they be able to relate to the characters?

- Is there anything in it that is unnecessary—anything that does not carry the story along?

- Is the punctuation about right?

- Are the lengths of sentences about right?

- Are the lengths of paragraphs varied, and about right?

- Are the words too complicated?

- Does it have a smooth flow … introduction, middle and conclusion?

Apply this questionnaire to your story when you have finished it!

Use this questionnaire for each of your stories. It will help keep you on the right track!

Now, let's get down to the most enjoyable part—writing your short story or novel, using all the guidelines you have learned up to this point.

Chapter 13 Bringing It All Together

This is the fun bit. It's where you bring your characters and their dialogue into the setting you created, and add the conflict we talked about earlier. These components of your story now all come together.

And it is here you will appreciate the value of giving so much attention to developing those special people in your story. Here you will appreciate the minute detail to your setting, and to your plot.

Your story can be any length, but it should be long enough for the conflict to be resolved in an acceptable way. Well, acceptable to the reader, at least. It may not necessarily have to be resolved to the same extent we would like it to be fixed up in our own private lives.

Your story should be long enough for the characters to be able to fully develop, there should be no loose ends at the time, leaving your readers asking themselves … 'well, so what … what was that all about?'

So far we have looked at all the ingredients of creative writing—theme, point of view, the characters, their dialogue—who says what and how and to whom, where the story is set and so on.

But good writing is never a block of each of these components standing alone.

Your job as a creative writer writing your story is to tie each of those aspects together in the cleverest way possible, to weave the theme through the characters, to bring the characters together with the setting, and show how they act, and why, and how they grate on each others nerves. It is your job to show your readers that you have created a story that they will really want to read. It is in your creativity that they will turn to time after time to get the entertainment they want in their reading. This might even be your very first story or novel. If it's really good, and let's hope it will be, then they will look for your name on stories and books in the future. Now isn't that something worthwhile to aim for with your writing? It sure is!

If you please your reader with originality, you have succeeded. If you don't, then you will have failed.

Chapter 14 Self Publishing

What if you can't get those great stories or that novel published? You know they are good. Your friends, who have been really critical and have told you the truth about them, have told you that they are great, and they really enjoyed them. And you know that what you have written is good. And still you can't get anyone to publish them. How sad.

Well, it's not the end of the world for writers. As I said in the beginning of this book, writing is not easy. And neither is getting fiction published.

This is where modern technology is increasingly becoming a writer's real friend.

Self publishing, using the print-on-demand services of printers, and the increasing popularity of e-books, are proving very popular. With the recent demise of so many bookshops around the world, and with the decrease in publishing activity by so many well-established publishing houses, and the reduction in publishing by many magazines, the openings for many works of fiction, even for established writers, have almost disappeared.

Consider print-on-demand publishing for your novel, or your collection of short stories.

You write the story—however long—and you design the pages of your book, and design a cover, and submit it to one such publisher.

If you are creative with your writing, and in other areas of your life too, you might be able to design the pages yourself. If you can't, you can get someone with appropriate software to do the typesetting for you.

Or the printer might have contractors who can do just that for you and get your book professionally set up for printing.

Here's a big hint. Get a quote first, and see just what the company is offering. Some will want several thousands dollars to get your book into twenty-five thousand bookshops around the world and indeed, they will even offer the world itself. In reality, they might offer the book to all those bookshops, but that is not the same as each of those twenty-five thousand bookshops actually stocking your book and selling it and paying you royalties.

Print-on-demand services vary. One I have found to be consistently good, very economical and that provides all writers and artistic creators with the standard of professionalism they deserve, is Lulu (www.lulu.com). They are based in America, but, thanks to the versatility of the Internet, this does not stop anyone from anywhere else in the world from using their service.

HOW DOES IT WORK?

You write the manuscript. It could be a collection of short stories, or a whole novel. You convert the manuscript into PDF format, set up an account with, say, Lulu , and upload the PDF as a single file, and the cover too as a separate file. Look at Lulu's site. There are so many options, depending on whether you want Lulu to act as publisher, in which case they will provide you with the ISBN and the bar code that must be placed on the back cover, and will set up a Spotlight page to help you promote your book. You will, of course, still have to promote your book in any way you think appropriate, and hope for the revenue to come in and reward you for your troubles and efforts. Your book will even be available as an e-book, so readers will be able to download it.

With Lulu, the only requirement for this service, assuming you do the design work of the cover and the typography yourself, is that you buy one copy.

You will need to get your own ISBN and get a bar code if you act as the publisher. You should also get the cataloguing-in-production data from the national library in your country, and send that same library some copies for their holdings. The library will then get your book listed in the current books in print data bases, and this is essential to any book sales.

That's it. You can buy any number of books you want.

Other print-on-demand printers will charge a lot more, and they might do a lot more, or at least they will tell you that they will. But I have learned to become very sceptical about the claims some of them will make. But check them all out, because what suits me might not be the service you think will work for your book.

With any book, much of the demand for the book comes from the type of book, and how it is promoted. But I must warn you, there is no guarantee you will sell anything like the numbers of books you had hoped to. You might sell one copy. You might sell none. You mighty sell thousands. But who knows? It all depends on the marketing you give it.

Chapter 15 Over to You

And that's all there is to writing fiction ... writing your story.

All good writing is about that magical ingredient in life—personal achievement. It's what you want to get out of the process of putting words together to make a meaningful story—your story.

This book can only give you the basics of the process. The rest is up to you.

Good writing comes with difficulty to all (well, nearly all) writers. Be patient. Be prepared to re-work your writing as often as you need to. Be prepared to spend a lot of time getting your story just the way you wanted it. Not all are so gifted they can write one draft, send it to the publisher and get by return mail a publishing contract. It seldom works that way. If only! I am sure we would all turn into very good writers.

But that doesn't mean that you can't continually improve your craft. Write as often as you can. Write from the heart.

Write it as you feel inspired. Write it as the urge overwhelms you to put words down on paper (or into your computer these days). But just put the words down ... anywhere.

And with that constant striving for improvement, that's just what you will achieve. Even if you aim for small incremental improvements to your writing each time, just imagine how much that amounts to over a year or two. Perhaps you can aim for slightly larger incremental improvements. That's even better.

But all good writers seem to have one thing in common. They believe in themselves. It's what they want to do, usually above all else. And they won't accept anything less than their goal.

That's really what makes a good writer. So go for it.

And good luck in creating your story!

Index

Index

www.ingramcontent.com/pod-product-compliance
Lightning Source LLC
Chambersburg PA
CBHW070903280326

41934CB00008B/1562